WHITE COLLAR FACTORY
A MINIGRAPH

White Collar Factory: A Minigraph

FifthMan
c/o Allford Hall Monaghan Morris
Morelands, 5-23 Old Street
London EC1V 9HL, UK

ISBN
978-0-9934378-5-4

First published in 2017 by FifthMan

Editor: Emma Keyte

CONTENTS

TWO
SIMONS

SIMON SILVER
DERWENT LONDON

Derwent Valley (later to become Derwent London) was established as a property company in 1984. It originated from a Yorkshire property holding which included four hundred yards of railway track servicing a Shell depot, using a steam engine now housed in the National Railway Museum in York. In fact, an image of the steam engine was used as our logo when the company was first formed. This is quite relevant because architecturally we have often been inspired by looking back over time and, in the same way that there is an honesty to those magnificent steam engines, so we have found the same sort of integrity with older industrial buildings.

Our passion for architecture really took off in 1987 when we acquired Colebrook & Wilmar Estates, a private property company whose portfolio included a small number of workshop buildings in Colebrooke Row in Islington and a rather wonderful Art Deco-type light industrial building called Middlesex House in Fitzrovia, which the company still owns.

The Use Class Order was revised at that time, permitting the automatic conversion of light industrial buildings to offices. This created a great opportunity to convert our holdings into a new type of contemporary office space. It was also at this time that we were introduced to a young firm of architects, Troughton McAslan, who taught us the importance of volume and light. These industrial buildings all benefitted from generous proportions, far greater than the average office building, and therefore offered our architects incredible potential. The results of the conversions were stunning; it was a moment that was to influence Derwent far into the future and our immediate response was to attempt to find other interesting factory buildings that would yield similar opportunities.

Our appetite grew and our search for industrial buildings in London saw us purchase the former Army & Navy Depository in Victoria where we converted 180,000 square feet in two adjoining buildings, Gordon and Greencoat House, in 1990. We then migrated east and in 1991 purchased the former Companies House in City Road now known as Oliver's Yard, and Morelands in Old Street in 1992. It was at Morelands that that we first met four precocious young architects whom we have worked with ever since. Their firm, Allford Hall Monaghan Morris, is today prized among the architectural elite and now numbers around 350!

Perhaps one of the most significant former industrial buildings in our portfolio is the Tea Building which we purchased in 2000. Originally a warehouse of 240,000 square feet, it was comprehensively regenerated together with AHMM and is now a thriving community of tenants from the creative industries as well as home to Shoreditch House, who have their swimming pool on our roof.

So the industrial aesthetic became part of our DNA. So much so that David Rosen, our specialist agent, Simon Allford and I used to frequently discuss the prospect of one day building a different type of office building. It would be on an industrial scale, with a design that would offer the same advantages we had experienced in all these wonderful buildings. Twenty or so years ago it was something of a dream but today White Collar Factory is a reality.

The catalyst was our merger with London Merchant Securities in 2007. They owned a group of tired 1960s buildings fronting Old Street Roundabout that were ripe for redevelopment. A year of brainstorming sessions between us and AHMM, Arup, AECOM, AKT II and Jackson Coles resulted in the idea of a new and progressive type of office building with generous floor plates, floor-to-ceiling heights of 3.5 metres, opening windows and a passive cooling system assisted by the expressed concrete frame that would retain either 'coolth' or warmth just like the industrial buildings of the past. The only minus was the loss of floor space in storey levels due to the incredible volumes that were being proposed. However, the pluses far outweighed the minuses: surely floors with generous cubic capacity would prove more valuable in the long term?

So we built a fully functioning, all-singing and all-dancing prototype to test our theories and in 2014 the demolition of our older buildings commenced.

The result is a Jean Prouvé-inspired, factory-type building for white collar office workers. White Collar Factory is the most progressive office building to be constructed in central London in terms of design and function – indeed many of our leases exclude the need for dilapidations – but it is also a new place in the city: Old Street Yard offers new public realm and a series of re-made low-rise buildings that will house a number of smaller companies and three restaurants that will serve not only the 2,500 new occupants, but also the local community.

SIMON ALLFORD
ALLFORD HALL MONAGHAN MORRIS

'Gentlemen, we have run out of money. It's time to start thinking'.
Ernest Rutherford

These were not the exact words that Simon Silver and Paul
Williams used in autumn 2008 when we began talking about a new
collaboration. As a REIT (real estate investment trust), Derwent
London knew their well-let property portfolio, despite FTSE panic,
was built on solid footings. But the general direction was clear and
we were all excited by the idea that innovation might flourish in a
(financial) crisis.

At the time, we were working together on the Angel Building, the
fifth in a series of major projects with Derwent which led us from
Morelands to the Johnson Building to Horseferry House, with the
Tea Building running alongside as a constant testbed. Through
these projects and study tours of New York, Chicago, the midwest
and west coast (as well as almost all of London), we had all long
since committed to the delights of exposed concrete, the engine
that drove our particular architectural adventure in space, light
and volume.

By 2008 we were agreed that our research had to go to the next
level of detail. The consultant team, led on our side by Steve Taylor
and Adam Burgess, created the base case of an idealised office.
It was of five storeys with a central core, good floor-to-ceiling
heights, facade glazing adjusted in response to the solar load,
a masonry facade and natural ventilation assisted by an emerging
idea of cold water pipes embedded in the inevitable concrete frame
– which itself would provide the finish. This was not a building
that any of us intended to make, but it was the ultimate test of
the minimal design, divorced from the particularities of site and
reflective of our interest in the theory of convergence: that nothing
need be added, nothing could be taken away, and that everything
must work hard and do more than one thing.

The name 'White Collar Factory' was not coined until December
2010 at my wedding, in a conversation between me, Paul Finch
and David Rosen: architecture and life are endlessly intertwined!
It was about then that our generic idea also moved to a specific
place – a site in Old Street.

The challenges of engaging with this urban block's rich past,
and the location of the roundabout, enriched the White Collar

Factory story. This recognition of the import of history of place and indeed the history we share with Derwent – one of reuse and reinvention – is reflected in the retention of two buildings, one as incubator offices, and the other as three loft apartments, both over generous ground floor units. Why get rid of a good structure? The vestiges of the base case study can be seen in the two new-build studio buildings, anchored to a supercore that opportunistically travels through the salvaged steel frame of the incubator. A new residential building reflects our shared interest in the cultural, social and financial benefits of a mixed-use urban building.

To the north of the site the case study took on its most extreme development. The consent for a tower by others – won in appeal – that came with the acquisition of the site allowed us to set a new precedent for height. The six conceptual floors became sixteen, and we suggested the great French metalworker and builder Jean Prouvé as our shared key reference for how we might make a visually solid yet lightweight facade. The resulting system, like any good system, is endlessly adapted, at ground level, at the sky, to the four points of the compass and halfway up.

The principles of the new White Collar Factory define this collection of six buildings, which themselves define Old Street Yard - a new piece of city on the edge of the old City of London.

When we stood in the concrete atrium on the completion of the Angel Building, Simon Silver remarked that we might never top that project. Ever the optimist, I remarked that we had better do so, and at Old Street! History will be the judge. But at White Collar Factory we have built an idea and remained true to the ambitions we set ourselves. By learning from the buildings we have recycled and reinvented, we have established a new paradigm for how to build, finish and let an office. We have also built a new place in the city. And of course now, as we move on to a new collaboration at Soho Place, we retain similar ambitions, building on the nine years of research and construction that have made White Collar Factory.

WHITE COLLAR FACTORY IN EIGHT MINUTES

THE STORY OF WHITE COLLAR
FACTORY BEGINS IN THE
NINETEENTH CENTURY, WHEN
FACTORIES AND WAREHOUSES
WERE BUILT AS THE STAGE SET
FOR THE NEW MANUFACTURING
INDUSTRIES GROWING OUT OF
THE INDUSTRIAL REVOLUTION.

The new factories, despite often being dangerous places to work, were buildings of quality, robust and flexible structures with high ceilings and large windows. Their quality was such that many are still in use today, not always for manufacturing, but as homes, schools, shops and places of work, and as factories for the new technology based industries of the twenty-first century.

Allford Hall Monaghan Morris (AHMM) and Derwent London are the designers and developers behind several of these reinvented factory buildings, and a number of other building transformations which celebrate the factory aesthetic. These successful projects raised new questions: why are nineteenth-century warehouse and factory buildings so good at being twenty-first century offices? What exactly is so good about them? And, could we build better – and increase investment returns – by adopting some of these characteristics in modern buildings?

During 2008, with the economy in recession, AHMM and Derwent London began a research project to explore what could be learned from these industrial precedents. This investigation led first to a baseline model and a set of five principles for building what would become a White Collar Factory.

The baseline model is for a 'long life, loose fit, low energy' building which has an extended lifespan, a place in the city for the factory workers of today which will adapt to future uses that can't yet be predicted. The building does more with less – so, for example, the walls provide the enclosure, solar shading and insulation but also a finish. It provides its own climate control by passive means where possible, supplemented by intelligent features adaptable to future technologies. By stripping everything back to the raw components, and doing these really well, it was possible to create a workspace which was flexible and generic, but with a very special character and quality.

The baseline White Collar Factory concept is a six-storey building with a 45-metre square plan, a central core and a four-metre floor-to-floor height. The skin and concrete structure are integrated, so there are no perimeter columns, giving punched openings and simple windows. The facade is equally simple. The generic model has a Category A base build with raised-floor power and data, and standard soffit-slung light fittings, but comes with a shopping list of optional extras such as enhanced light fittings and on-floor shower and WC facilities, and a net-to-gross ratio of 81 per cent.

White Collar Factory ## generic design

(A) building height G(5m) + 5 storeys (E) central core (I) typical floor NIA:GIA = 85-87% (M) section 20 does not apply

(B) 45 x 45 m floor plate (F) GIA = 130,000 sqft (J) Wall to floor ratio = 0.35 (N) limited sub divisible floors

(C) 4m floor to floor = tall ceilings (G) NIA = 105,300 sqft (K) No basement, car park or transfer structure (O) 1 or 2 tenancies

(D) 9m x 9m insitu concrete frame (H) overall NIA:GIA = 81% (L) Min. fresh air and radiant slabs (P) 8 WC's per floor

= £165 per sqft

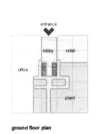
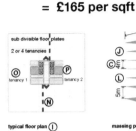
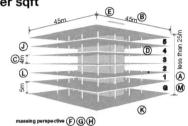

ground floor plan   typical floor plan (I)   massing perspective (F)(G)(H)

key   facade modules

Office   lifts   stairs

retail   plant / servicing   WC's

lobby / reception   circulation   optional extra WC's

grande | 30% glazing   regular | 53% glazing   skinny | 66% glazing

White Collar Factory ## section

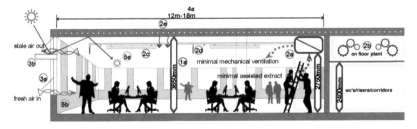

(1) tall ceilings = (1a) 3650mm floor to ceiling heights (3) passive low tech facade = (3a) opening windows

(2) smart servicing = (2a) minimal fresh air mech. vent with extract from bulkhead (3b) external shading where needed (south, east and west facing, if not overshadowed)

(2b) on floor plant (4) deep plan = (4a) generous scale provides best opportunity for greatest market share

(2c) light fittings included as basic product (5) concrete structure = (5a) exposed concrete soffit

(2d) power & data soffit mounted

(2e) radiant slab for cooling & heating (5b) concrete perimeter upstand increases structural spans and eliminates perimeter columns

The five principles of the generic model, which can be applied to any specific site, are:

TALL CEILINGS

Generous volumes increase the possibilities for future use wherever the market leads. Natural daylight penetrates far into the floorplate, while artificial lighting is evenly distributed across the space. The physics of the stack effect mean that, with warm air rising, the internal temperature is more likely to remain comfortable for the users, and the airier space contributes to their sense of wellbeing.

SMART SERVICING

Passive systems are maximised: cold water pipes are cast in situ in the radiant concrete slab, which provides cooling through its thermal mass, and natural daylight and fresh air are invited in. There is no excessive 'kit', although tenants can upgrade their individual spaces.

SIMPLE PASSIVE FACADE

The facade is glazed where it counts – above desk height – and is fitted with openable windows so that users can get fresh air when they want it. Shading is provided where necessary, and responds to the context. Similarly, the amount of glazing varies to suit the orientation of the building – most of it is to the north, there is less to the west and east, and least of all to the south elevation.

DEEP PLAN

The generous scale of the floorplates offers the best opportunity for the greatest market share. Each floor can be split between tenants, and optional voids between floors help to connect larger, multi-floor tenancies. A compact central core supports good net-to-gross and wall-to-floor ratios.

CONCRETE STRUCTURE

The structure carries Concrete Core Cooling (or CCC – chilled water circulating through pipes embedded in the floor slabs), and has a high, active thermal mass to help condition the office space. Exposed, the concrete structure replaces the need for decorating and has a durable and pleasing contemporary aesthetic.

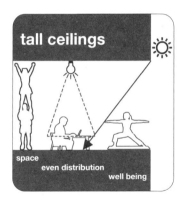

tall ceilings

space
even distribution
well being

smart servicing

minimal provision
upgradable
passive systems

simple passive facade

glazing where it counts
natural ventilation when you want it
solar shading where its needed

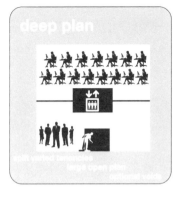

deep plan

split varied tenancies
large open plan
perimeter aisle

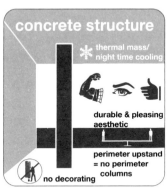

concrete structure

thermal mass/ night time cooling

durable & pleasing aesthetic

perimeter upstand = no perimeter columns

no decorating

The five design principles developed during the research study.

Derwent London had, as part of its merger with LMS in 2007, acquired a large site at the corner of City Road and Old Street, overlooking 'Silicon Roundabout' – named for the fast-growing cluster of technology companies starting up in the area as the recession hit. To test the ideas in the generic model and to launch the idea to prospective tenants, a scheme of six buildings, including a White Collar Factory, was developed and a prototype constructed on site. To realistically test the system, a £1 million prototype factory was built in the sky, jacked up on stilts above a redundant service yard. Essentially a 325 square-metre slice of White Collar Factory, it had the big spans, openable windows, large volumes, concrete core cooling and robust construction developed in the baseline model. It was built by Multiplex, the preferred main contractor for the project, using the likely supply chain and management team. The prototype stood on site for twelve months from 2013 to 2014, its performance data recorded and analysed by the engineers, Arup, before being dismantled to make way for the next iteration of the White Collar story, a White Collar campus. The value of building the prototype was clear to all: a benefit of knowing the client well (and the client knowing themselves), it enabled the design team to test the details in a 1:1 working mock-up and gave more certainty when work began on the full scheme.

The idea of a new place in the city was the single aspect of the White Collar concept that could not be tested by prototype or baseline model, and yet is central to the success of the initiative. Working outwards from the theoretical models, White Collar Factory needed now to be adapted to context. At Old Street, it would need to reflect the spirit of growth, energy, creativity and urban change that identifies this neighbourhood, as well as responding to the very specific constraints of the site.

The result is a campus of buildings which take up a whole city block, but at the same time make it newly permeable with the introduction of a central public space: Old Street Yard. To the south, two existing buildings have been retained, refurbished and extended as street-corner 'bookends', with infill buildings added to give a consistent yet varied perimeter to the block. These smaller-scale buildings have a mixture of restaurant, retail, 'studio office' and residential space and, with the landscaped courtyard, provide the setting for their big sister: the new-build, sixteen-storey White Collar Factory which overlooks Old Street roundabout.

External and internal views of the built prototype.

This factory tower adopts all the principles of the baseline and prototype models, with the 53 by 41 metre floor plan adapted to suit the context, site footprint, rights to light and orientation. The building height (sixteen storeys rather than the baseline model's six) required additional structure, services and sprinklers, along with a basement.

Applying the findings of the White Collar Factory study has resulted in a building which is theoretically 10-15 per cent more efficient to build and uses 25 per cent less energy than a typical new city office building, and this performance continues to be monitored. It brings together crafted elements with machine-built components. The higher floor-to-ceiling heights sacrifice lettable square footage for more valuable space with natural light. It stands in a campus which is granular rather than corporate, contextual rather than curated, reflecting the neighbourhood in which it sits. The internal aesthetic is sufficiently rich that tenants do not have to do so much with their fit-out: even the unfinished floors feel like characterful places rather than empty shells. It provides just those things which are needed: nothing is redundant.

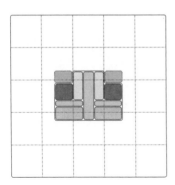
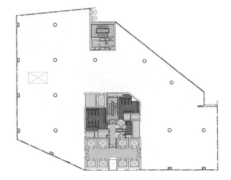

From research to reality: the generic White Collar Factory plan (left) and the plan as built at Old Street.

CITY SECTION
THROUGH WHITE COLLAR FACTORY
AND OLD STREET YARD

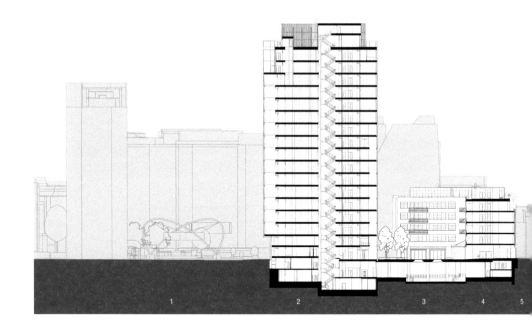

1   Old Street roundabout
2   White Collar Factory
3   Old Street Yard courtyard & basement studio
4   Old Street Yard low-rise buildings
5   Featherstone Street

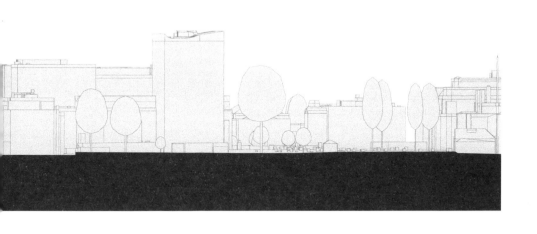

PLAN
GROUND
1:1250

1	Courtyard	7	Loading bay	13	Building 5 office
2	White Collar Factory entrance hall	8	Building 2 retail/restaurant	14	Building 6 residential
3	Cafe	9	Building 3 retail/restaurant	15	Entrance to basement cycle store
4	Lift lobby	10	Reception (for buildings 2, 3 and 4)	16	Old Street roundabout
5	Office	11	Passage		
6	Old Street reception	12	Building 4 retail/restaurant		

PLAN

1   Factory floorplate
2   South core
3   North core
4   Building 2 office
5   Building 3 office
6   Building 4 office

7   Supercore (for buildings 2, 3 and 4)
8   Building 5 apartments
9   Building 6 apartments

PLAN
LEVEL 10 (TYPICAL UPPER FLOOR)
1:1250

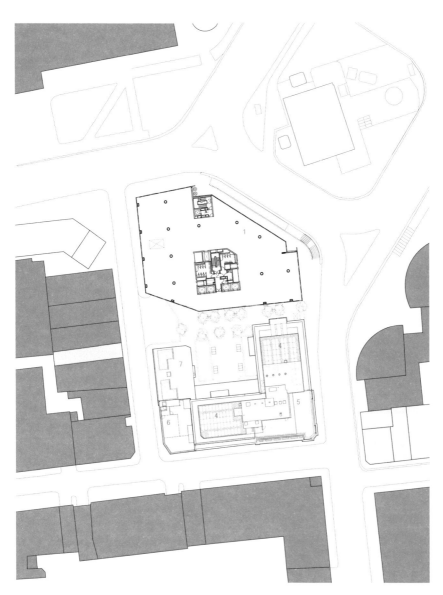

1   Factory floorplate
2   South core
3   North core
4   Photovoltaic panels above plant
5   Building 3 (roof terrace below)
6   Building 5 (roof terraces below)

7   Building 6 (roof terraces below)

PLAN

1   Rooftop bar
2   External terrace
3   Running/BMU track
4   Plant

ELEVATION
WEST
1:1250

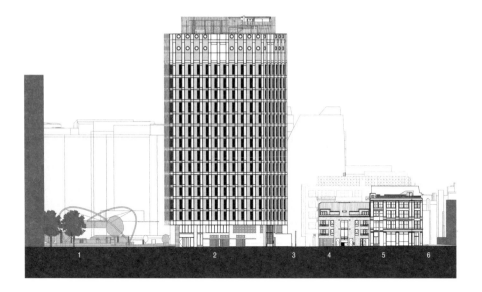

1   Old Street roundabout
2   White Collar Factory
3   Entrance to courtyard and loading bay
4   Building 6
5   Building 5
6   Featherstone Street

ELEVATION

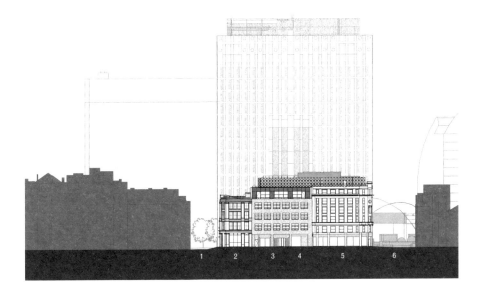

1   Mallow Street
2   Building 5
3   Building 4
4   Passageway to courtyard
5   Building 3
6   City Road

1
OLD
STREET
YARD

DESIGN THINKING

MANY ARCHITECTS INSPIRED BY THE INDUSTRIAL AESTHETIC SOUGHT TO MAXIMISE THE EFFICIENCY OF THEIR BUILDINGS BY INTEGRATING STRUCTURE, SKIN AND SYSTEMS.

LEARNING BY INSPIRATION

White Collar Factory is not the first building to be inspired by industrial structures, and looking at buildings which took their lead from nineteenth-century warehouses provided valuable inspiration. Normally, structure, skin and systems are designed independently, but by bringing them together a building can become much smarter. Servicing can be integrated into the structure, which can then be minimised, and the skin designed in turn to minimise the servicing required.

Jean Prouvé is the most significant among the designers of such buildings, with his background as an architect, metalworker and maker. He could see that industrial buildings stood the test of time; they reflected the processes in their construction and the possibilities – and limitations – of machine making. It is his appreciation of the hand crafted and the machine made, and the way that he brought these two approaches together in his building, that makes him so resonant as an inspiration for the design of White Collar Factory.

Jean Prouvé; the Maison Tropicale prototype photographed outside the Tate Modern in London, 2008.

He was interested in how an integrated structure and skin could help to condition the internal space in response to context and orientation. With his Maison Tropicale he investigated how this could be done – at very little cost – to solve the problem of a building shortage in France's African colonies. The parts were manufactured in a factory in Nancy from folded sheet metal and flown to Niger, where the house was constructed by just two men. The outer walls help to shade the inner room, which opens onto the verandah-like space around it. The walls of the inner room have multiple panels perforated with miniature glazed portholes, this circular shape favoured above a square because circles were easier to cut with a machine. The visual interest that such panels gave the exterior of his buildings (and the beautiful shadow patterns they created within) was a by-product of their primary, unified purpose as building envelope, sun screen and natural ventilation.

Frank Lloyd Wright is among the many other twentieth-century designers who explored how structure and enclosure could be integrated, and whose work the client and design teams visited in the United States during the development of White Collar Factory. Wright's Larkin Administration Building in Buffalo had pipework integrated into the structural columns, the air treated with a water mist to cool it as it filtered into the building.

Interior of the Larkin Building, Buffalo (Frank Lloyd Wright, 1906).

The structural, thermal and sculptural properties of concrete, as exploited by Louis Kahn, also provided material inspiration. At Kahn's Kimbell Art Museum in Texas, the concrete barrel vaults act as beams, freeing up the space below as well as forming a dynamic roofline. Each of the vaults is split along the top to let daylight into the galleries. The concrete itself is polished smooth and sits flush with the travertine infill surfaces. Kahn's highly refined use of concrete contrasts with that of Le Corbusier in his only North American building, the Carpenter Center for Visual Arts at Harvard University. Here the concrete is béton brut, poured using formwork of both steel and plywood to give a more tactile finish. At White Collar Factory, both boardmarked and polished concrete finishes are used throughout the building.

Late nineteenth and early twentieth-century factories and warehouses are characterised by their volume. Generous volume allows more to happen; height is just as important as area (for the occupants at least). It not only creates a sense of wellbeing, a space in which to grow, but it also offers flexibility. Plenty of space means a building has a built-in legacy. Frank Lloyd Wright's headquarters for Johnson Wax in Wisconsin is one such space – and was also visited by the team while researching White Collar Factory. Here, the deep-plan Great Workroom is lit from the perimeter and from the top, with huge tapered columns supporting the ceiling high above. It has been described as a cathedral of work, elevating industrial manufacturing processes and putting the worker first. As in many of Wright's buildings, it also brings something of the outside in, the tree-like columns taking their proportions from the natural environment.

Interior of the Johnson
Wax Headquarters, Racine,
Wisconsin (Frank Lloyd
Wright, 1939).

Industrial buildings tend to be expressive of their construction and their function – and the resulting forms can be extremely elegant. The hundreds of buildings designed by Albert Kahn for the Ford Motor Company all show a thorough understanding of the processes involved with car manufacture, and speak eloquently of these processes.

View of the blast furnaces and the south and west facades of the Ford Motor Company's Open Hearth Mills at the Rouge River Plant, Dearborn, Michigan (Albert Kahn, 1926-36).

Mies van der Rohe used Albert Kahn's factory spaces to explain his idea of universal space. In a famous collage he superimposed coloured planes onto an image of Kahn's aircraft assembly building for Glenn L Martin to represent an ensemble of components that could be rearranged to suit changing demands of the space. The factory, with its elegant proportions and logical structural framework, became a flexible enclosure which would allow any kind of activity to happen inside. Many of Mies' early projects demonstrate this concept, including SR Crown Hall at the Illinois Institute of Technology (IIT), which was intended to be a 'home for ideas and adventures', appropriated by programmes yet to be defined.

SR Crown Hall, Illinois Institute of Technology (Mies van der Rohe, 1956); Project for a Concert Hall, collage showing an interior perspective (Mies van der Rohe, 1942).

A combination of volume, honesty and structural rigour results in buildings with extremely flexible shells. They can deal with change within and without, elements can be added and some taken away, but the basic structure remains sustainable: it has an inherent value that will survive. The Van Nelle Fabriek (1931) is a vast factory in Rotterdam designed by Leendert van der Vlugt.

During its early lifetime it was a food processing plant, but when it ceased to operate in the 1990s it was refurbished as a home for creative and media start-ups. While its external appearance still tells the story of these earlier manufacturing processes, the internal spaces are more than robust enough to cope with its current use – and potential future uses.

Exterior and interior, Van Nelle Design Factory, Rotterdam (Leendert van der Vlugt, 1931, then Wessel de Jonge, 2004).

Jean Prouvé took the idea of flexibility one step further with his demountable buildings and furniture which inspired the White Collar Factory approach. As a metalworker, he looked at the potential of folded sheet metal to produce components which could be cheaply manufactured and easily assembled into buildings. These prefabricated buildings were intended to address the housing shortage in France, and Prouvé's La Maison des Jours Meilleurs (1956) was constructed in response to an appeal from clergyman Abbé Pierre after a woman froze to death on the streets of Paris. Built in just two days, the prototype was intended to prompt the mass production of similar homes. It was constructed of a prefabricated steel unit containing kitchen and bathroom, enclosed by wood panels and aluminium slabs, and sitting on a concrete base. Prouvé's demountables also inspired the units developed by AHMM for the fit-out of The Office Group's space in White Collar Factory, discussed later in this book.

Maison de l'abbé Pierre (or La Maison des Jours Meilleurs), Paris (Jean Prouvé, 1955).

LEARNING BY PRECEDENT

AHMM's first warehouse collaboration with Derwent was the practice's own office – Morelands – further down Old Street. Hidden a block back from the main road, the lightly refurbished building has proved flexible enough for several changes in tenancy. As a mini White Collar Factory, it has adapted to the growth of the practice with the addition of a new upper floor and roof terrace, and continues to reinvent itself. The shaded courtyards between front and back buildings give a sense of place and privacy.

Street and courtyard
views of Morelands,
Old Street.

Tea Building, like Morelands, has been an organic project, with a series of interventions made over time in response to fluctuations in the property market and the evolving workstyles of the users. The building – in fact, a complex of three warehouses – was used for curing bacon and tea storage in its previous lives and sits in the heart of Shoreditch. A reinvention based on minimal expenditure and very slight interventions have effectively made the building undemolishable: tenants enjoy the robustness, generosity and inherent flexibility of the space, which grows and changes with them on an ongoing basis.

Exterior of Tea Building,
Shoreditch High Street.

Following on from Tea, the refurbishment of the Johnson Building in 2006 was aimed at the more corporate market in London's 'Midtown', between the City and the West End. An early twentieth-century building in Hatton Garden, London's jewellery quarter, was knitted together with new-build office floors by a central 'city room'. Rather than having the excessive finish typical of many speculative schemes, the scheme broke the rules by relying on the building's structure and natural materials to give the new address its character. It was also the first Derwent building to use the more passive displacement air conditioning. Horseferry House, a 1930s former government office in Westminster, was also refurbished around the idea of city rooms – in this case, two redundant lightwells. These, one open and one enclosed with ETFE (ethylene tetrafluoroethylene) cushions, are now the circulation cores of the building, bright spaces so that any journey through the building goes through a daylit room.

While the Johnson Building and Horseferry House were more sophisticated refurbishments than the light touch treatments of Morelands and Tea, all were connected by the recurring themes of working with what was already there, doing more with less and bringing the city inside. A fifth project with Derwent, Angel Building in Islington, followed a similar strategy. An unloved and rather antisocial 1980s building was stripped back to its frame, extended and remodelled to reflect the northern sweep of St John Street. The materials chosen once again had more than one function – here, the concrete provided structure, thermal mass and internal finishes. The former car park in the centre of the original building was relined and covered to form an atrium and, by pushing the reception and security line right back from the front door, became a true public space. Between street and desk many things happen: a cafe, art, breakout spaces and promenade.

Exterior and interior of
Angel Building, Islington.

THE WHITE COLLAR CAMPUS IS
NOT JUST A PIECE OF RESEARCH;
IT IS A PIECE OF CITY. THE
CREATION OF A NEW COMMUNITY
OF USERS WAS AN INTEGRAL
PART OF THE PROJECT. AS A
'UNIVERSAL SPACE' THESE USERS
ARE INVITED IN FROM THE CITY
AT LARGE, AS WELL AS FROM
THE BUILDINGS ON SITE.

Cities tend to grow organically, so making a new piece of city was a particular challenge, not least because Old Street was never a village like its neighbours Clerkenwell and Shoreditch. It was always a crossroads rather than a place, a waymark to be passed through on the way to somewhere else.

White Collar Factory sits right at the junction where Old Street meets City Road on the northern fringe of the City of London. Old Street is an ancient route, first recorded in around 1200, which ran from east to west outside the walls of the city and connected with the old Roman roads to York and Colchester. It met Royal Row, a major route north from the city gates, close to the natural spring at St Agnes Well. By the mid-eighteenth century the area had become known for its pleasure gardens and baths, as well as the military training grounds of Bunhill Fields and the Artillery Ground, the two separated by a narrow strip of land used as a burial place for victims of the plague.

In 1761, the new City Road was built linking Islington to the north with Royal Row (which also became known as City Road) and the City beyond and, despite the preservation of the Bunhill Fields burial ground, any remaining green space was gradually developed as the industrialising city expanded. Another new road – Featherstone Street – was constructed, which now marks the southern boundary of the White Collar Factory site. Old Street underground station opened in 1901, a final signal of the neighbourhood's urbanisation.

The streets surrounding the junction of Old Street and City Road retained their orthogonal layout right through until 1964, when the dense, Victorian feel of the area was drastically altered with the building of Old Street roundabout. This changed the urban grain, leaving certain older buildings – such as the 1930s commercial building which originally sat at the north-west corner of the White Collar Factory site – compromised in their setting, while more recent buildings – such as the slab-and-podium Transworld House on the north-east corner of the site, adjacent to the roundabout – embraced the new car-loving townscape.

1720

1755

1837

1897

1940

1964

1964

2009

1964

1964

The orthogonal grain of the Old Street area remained unchanged for two centuries until the building of Old Street roundabout in 1964. Fragments of the earlier grain were now artificially truncated by the new traffic island.

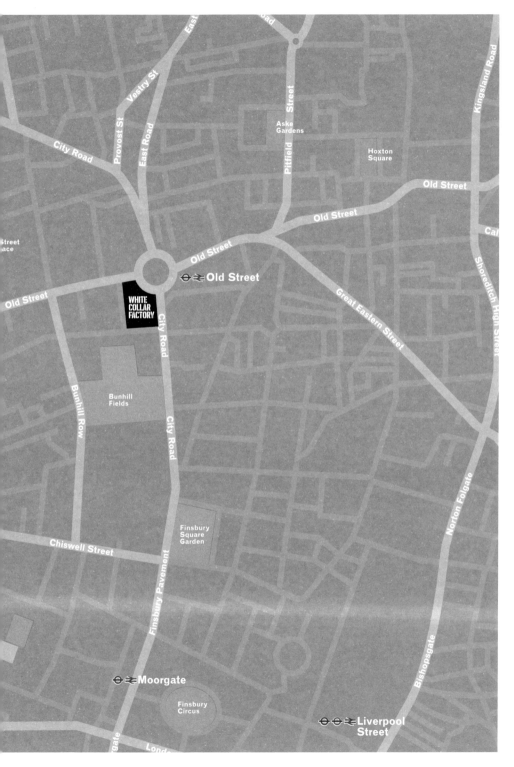

The White Collar campus challenges the car-focussed hierarchy of the roundabout. The old city block, bordered by Old Street, City Road, Featherstone Street and Mallow Street, with its new central courtyard, businesses, apartments and connecting alleyways, fixes the grain by offering a protected, pedestrian-first place away from the traffic, a new place in the city where people can stop and breathe. It is an antidote to harsher streetscape of the roundabout itself and suggests a secondary east-west route through the neighbourhood for those in the know.

The infill blocks around the south of the site are kept lower-rise to match the retained buildings and respect the Bunhill Row/Finsbury Square conservation area. Like the surrounding streets, the buildings line the street edges and have a fairly consistent cornice height. They share 'supercores', and at ground floor they have two front doors – one to the street and one to the central courtyard – which also act as thresholds to new spaces above and below. The White Collar Factory tower engages directly with the roundabout, its mass consistent with the larger buildings that mark the junction and its aesthetic reflecting the businesses of 'Tech City'.

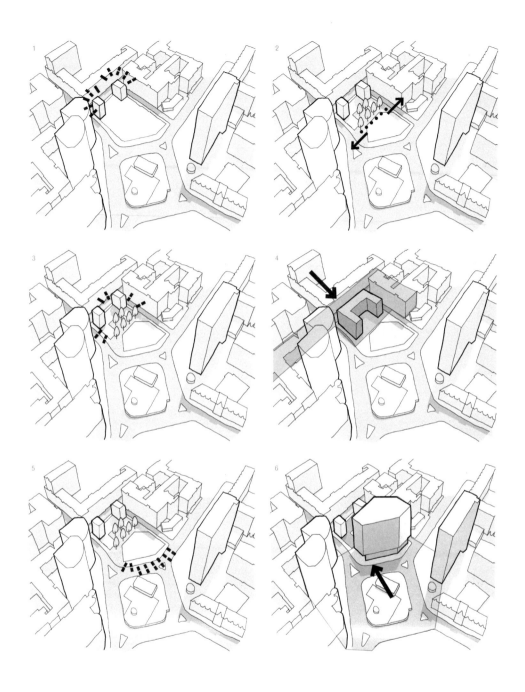

The planning strategy in sequence: buildings of merit on the southern corners of the site are retained (1); meaningful public realm is created at the heart of the development (2); infill blocks are introduced around the retained buildings (3); lower-rise offices including the refurbished, retained buildings redefine the Conservation Area (4); a new city block is established on Old Street roundabout (5); and the taller office block here creates a gateway to the site and redefines the roundabout (6).

ELEMENTS

A FUNDAMENTAL PRINCIPLE OF
WHITE COLLAR FACTORY IS TO
DO MORE WITH LESS, AND SO
THE ARCHITECTURE CELEBRATES
THE STRUCTURAL, THERMAL AND
PLASTIC PROPERTIES OF
CONCRETE. CONCRETE PROVIDES
THE STRUCTURE, IT CARRIES THE
SERVICING AND OFFERS
THERMAL MASS, AND IT GIVES
A HIGHLY EXPRESSIVE FINISH.

STRUCTURE + SERVICES + SKIN

BIM (Building Information Modelling) images showing structure (top left), servicing and plant (top right), and the full campus wrapped in its skin (above).

STRUCTURE

Concrete gives the building its structural frame in the form of columns, walls and floor slabs. The lift shafts and ceiling soffits are lined with smooth concrete, cast in plywood-lined metal shutters. However, in the important spaces, both inside and outside the building, the finish is far more expressive. Here, board-marked concrete is used to give a finely textured surface in a warm, light grey colour which gently reflects the light.

Research visits to the United States, and explorations in London too, provided an opportunity to look at the use of concrete in some seminal twentieth-century buildings.

Learning from America: Eero Saarinen's Morse and Ezra Stiles Halls (1961) and Gordon Bunshaft's Beinecke Library (1963) at Yale.

Expressive, purposeful, brutal concrete: The National Theatre in London (Denys Lasdun, 1976).

Traditionally, the formwork of timber shutters which gives board-marked concrete its distinctive texture was constructed on site by teams of carpenters using whatever materials were available. Now, shutters are generally made of steel or plywood. To save time on site at White Collar Factory, and negate the need for the timber shutter to be rebuilt after each casting, a rubber cast was taken from a bespoke timber mould, and then re-cast as a rubber liner which could be used over and over again.

Committing to concrete presented a series of design and construction challenges. With the concrete structure carrying the primary servicing as well as the pipes for core cooling there was no margin for error or retrofit: the concrete structure was the first thing to be built and it had to be detailed fully up-front. With large vertical surfaces to cast, the physical restrictions of working with concrete would be permanently expressed in the structure, manifested in the joint lines between each day's casting.

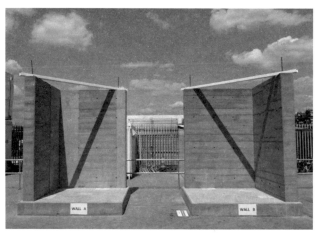

An initial set of twelve, metre-square mock-ups tested a series of recipes and shuttering types for the concrete. The differing mixes of cement, sand and aggregate gave a surprisingly broad palette of colours, and the two preferred finishes were then tested as larger 'walls'. These also tested how the concrete would be detailed: how external and internal corners would be expressed, and also the ends of walls and junctions between smooth and board-marked sections. A reusable rubber RECKLI mould was then cast from the chosen timber formwork.

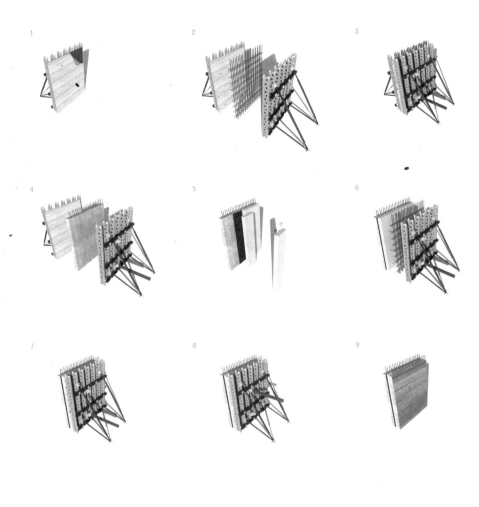

Casting the concrete: a standard shutter is constructed and the RECKLI rubber formwork is applied (1). Rebar (steel reinforcement) is put into place (2) and self-compacting concrete is pumped in to form the inner leaf (3). Once dry, the shuttering is removed (4) and a waterproof membrane and cavity insulation are added (5). Outer leaf rebar is put in place (6) and the concrete is poured again, pumped first from the base (7) then from high level (8). The pump connections and tie holes are sanded down or plugged to complete the finished wall (9).

WHITE COLLAR FACTORY - OLD STREET YARD
FLOOR PLATE - BUILDING 1

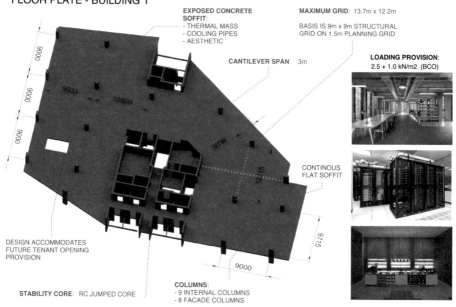

EXPOSED CONCRETE SOFFIT:
- THERMAL MASS
- COOLING PIPES
- AESTHETIC

MAXIMUM GRID: 13.7m x 12.2m

BASIS IS 9m x 9m STRUCTURAL GRID ON 1.5m PLANNING GRID

CANTILEVER SPAN: 3m

LOADING PROVISION:
2.5 + 1.0 kN/m2 (BCO)

CONTINOUS FLAT SOFFIT

DESIGN ACCOMMODATES FUTURE TENANT OPENING PROVISION

STABILITY CORE: RC JUMPED CORE

COLUMNS:
- 9 INTERNAL COLUMNS
- 8 FACADE COLUMNS

9000

9715

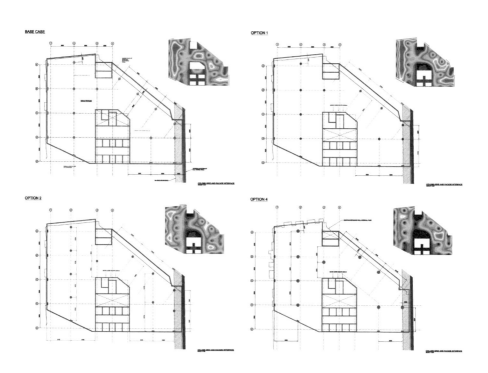

Engineering drawings by AKT II test varying scenarios for the column locations, and the resulting structural loads.

As a loose fit, long life building, White Collar Factory's structural frame is intended to last for over a century. It is flexible enough to withstand future changes in use or envelope, so there is a degree of sustainability built in. The ingredients for the concrete mix are also chosen to be from as sustainable sources as possible, and include ground-granulated blast-furnace slag (GGBS) and pulverised fuel ash (PFA) – by-products from steel-making and coal-fired power stations respectively. As well as lowering the embodied carbon footprint, the GGBS has an additional benefit of increasing the material durability of the concrete.

The irregular geometry of the Old Street site gave some freedom when defining the structural and planning grid of the floorplates. The column locations were optimised across the floorplates to balance structural efficiency with the inherent flexibility of the White Collar concept. The reinforced concrete slabs span up to twelve metres, aided by just five internal columns. These rely on connectivity into the central core with three-metre edge cantilevers to balance deflections.

Almost any development in central London has to cope with a complex subterranean landscape and White Collar Factory is no exception. Many services, including twin water mains, run under the east side of the building underneath City Road. At mid level are two large-bore rail tunnels driven through the London clay in 1901 and now maintained by Network Rail. A few years later another pair of rail tunnels was driven beneath, twenty metres below ground level. These tunnels were widened to form Old Street station, now on the London Underground's Northern Line.

New piles driven along the eastern perimeter of the White Collar tower would hit the edge of these tube tunnels, and even with the piles relocated it was critical to control and monitor ground movements around the tunnels. As a result, a cautious approach was taken with the foundations, and the basement excavation was dog-legged so the deepest part of the basement is furthest from the tunnels. The foundation piles were driven deep, past the London clay to rest on the firmer Thanet sands thirty metres below ground. The nearest pile is at least five metres clear of the nearest tunnel, and this meant incorporating a massive transfer structure into the basement. This takes the form of two very deep one-metre-thick concrete beams which transfer the loads from the outer columns of the tower back towards the centre and onto the piles.

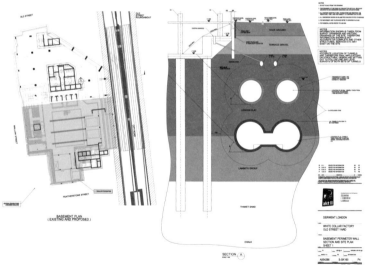

Foundation piles are driven during construction; engineer's section showing location of piles and underground tunnels.

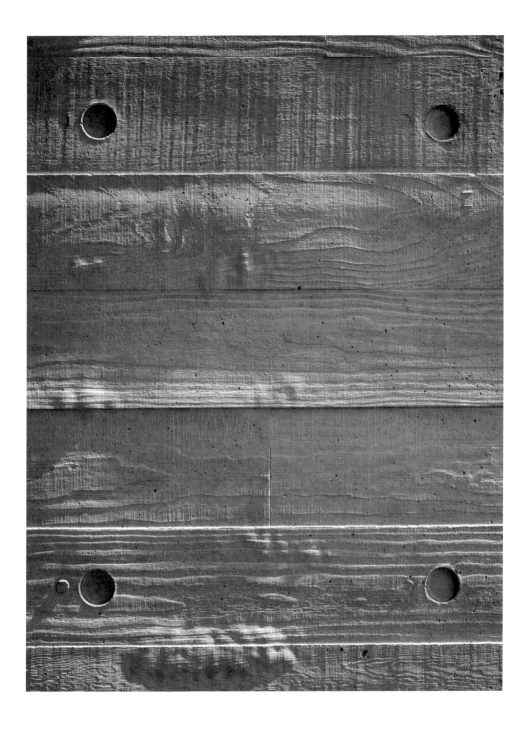

SERVICES

The architecture of White Collar Factory is designed to minimise the need for servicing: the spaces are cooled and ventilated where possible through passive means, and structure, services and skin are conceived as an integrated system. Where additional means of servicing are used, these are clearly expressed so that users understand exactly how their building lives and breathes.

The building has been the subject of a government-funded study into climate change mitigation, the outcomes of the study showing that because of the passive design features, the building will stand up to rising global temperatures over the next twenty to fifty years without the need for major material changes. It has achieved the UK's highest sustainability assessment rating of BREEAM Outstanding (and the USA's equivalent benchmark of LEED Platinum), within a normal construction budget and relying on passive measures rather than add-on technologies – credentials almost unprecedented for this scale of office development.

Cooling is primarily achieved through the concrete slab. Water is looped through pipework in the slab and the resulting 'coolth' radiates into the workspaces from the ceiling. The cold air sinks, to be replaced by warmer air which rises back up to the slab, where the heat is absorbed into the concrete. This combination of the activated slab and the optimised facade creates a stable, comfortable internal environment, which reduces the dependency on mechanical air conditioning, and requires less plant.

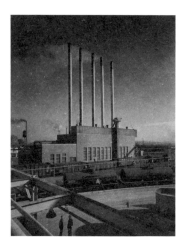

Albert Kahn's boiler house for B F Goodrich in Louisville, Kentucky (1914) is a frank expression of programme and servicing, with large areas of glazing exposing the machinery inside and a rank of slender chimneys.

Occupants can tap into additional cooling from sockets embedded in the soffit at strategic positions (such as in high load areas like meeting rooms or server suites) by simply connecting a pipe and running this to an additional radiant panel, like a domestic radiator. There are also 'heatwave boosters' around the perimeter which transform the existing trench heaters into trench coolers, with a cold water supply and small fan to push the cold air up into the work zone. All can be operated by the tenant.

Simple passive facades with openable windows are a fundamental principle of the White Collar Factory model. These windows, when open, naturally ventilate the office floors and help with cooling. Screens punched with Prouvé-inspired portholes help reduce the solar load, give protection from the wind and cast interesting shadows into the factory floors. Outside a certain range of temperatures, opening the windows will have a negative effect and overheat or overcool the space, and so traffic lights close to the lift lobby on each floor signal green to individual users (rather than facilities management) when opening them will have a positive benefit.

Sequence showing openable perforated ventilation panel. White Collar Factory has fully openable porthole windows, and traffic lights signal when these can be manually opened to cool the space.

The open windows will naturally ventilate to a distance of around six metres back from the facade, but this is a building with a deep plan, so there are two loops of ductwork – an inner and an outer ring – on each floor, bringing fresh, filtered air from roof level down into the space. The outer ring can be turned off when the perimeter windows are open for natural ventilation.

The base-build services are exposed on the ceiling, and can be adapted according to the tenant fit-out. The arrangement of services respects the planning grid, which is imagined across the soffit to enable cellular partitioning to be added without any retrofitting work. These services include air ducts, an intelligent lighting system which responds to daylight levels and movement, and a sprinkler system. User services are supplied from a raised access floor.

The building is divided into pairs of floors, and this double-height order is expressed on the facade. The pairings allow for connections to be built between floors should tenants take more than one level of the building (and are also expressed in a double-height space in front of the lift on every other floor). They also have a more practical purpose: fire protection, with each pair of floors forming a single fire compartment.

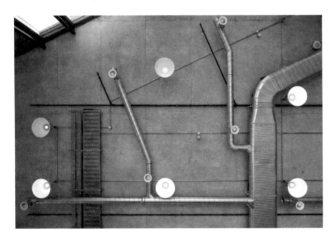

The base-build servicing includes larger steel duct feeds smaller 'branches' which deliver fresh air into the space. The slimmer galvanised lighting conduits are linked to detection points, and are supplemented by metal mesh cable trays. Pipework for the sprinkler system is left in the colour it wears as it leaves the factory: red oxide.

Solid black lines mark the division between each pair of floors on the facade.

SKIN

The skin of White Collar Factory brings together crafted and machined finishes to support the servicing strategy from first principles. 'Handmade' board-shuttered concrete wraps the building at pavement level, the close-up interest of the texture and detailing displaying the mark of the maker and giving it a more human scale as it meets the street. Above this, the envelope feels more efficient and machine-made. Glazing around the factory floors is interspersed with punched metal panels and banded with black aluminium panels which establish an order across each elevation. The tower is topped with a more refined layer of envelope which extends up to protect the rooftop running track. Above this an inner screen of cedar shields the roof plant and rooftop cafe.

There are subtle variances across the main elevations which express the internal programme – for example, the stair on the northern side of the building sits behind full-height glazing – and respond to the building's orientation. The principle of good daylighting is balanced against the need to keep sufficient sun out so that the building can be cooled passively. To this end the skin is an ever-changing system: to the south, east and west, glazing covers around a third of the facade to minimise the solar load; to the north, which receives little direct sunlight, glazing covers around two-thirds of the facade.

Like Peter Barefoot's glazed water tower and boiler house for Ipswich Hospital (1961), the White Collar tower is expressive of the activity inside.

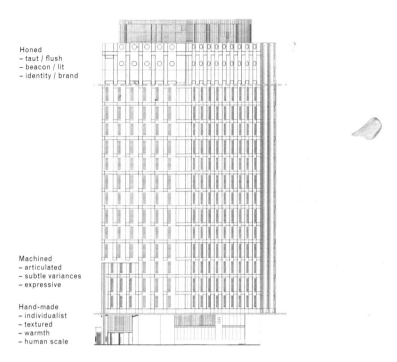

Honed
– taut / flush
– beacon / lit
– identity / brand

Machined
– articulated
– subtle variances
– expressive

Hand-made
– individualist
– textured
– warmth
– human scale

Early sketches exploring the texture of glazing and metal panels on each elevation; detail of the completed facade.

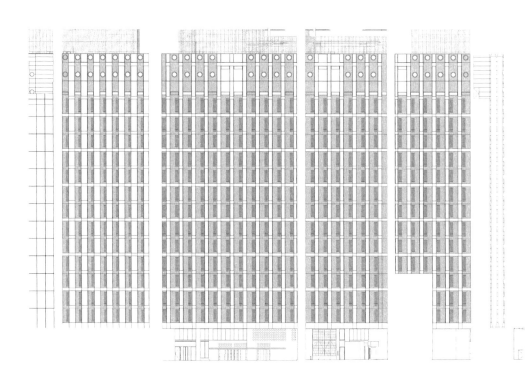

Unwrapped, the tower elevations show differing proportions of glazing according to orientation.

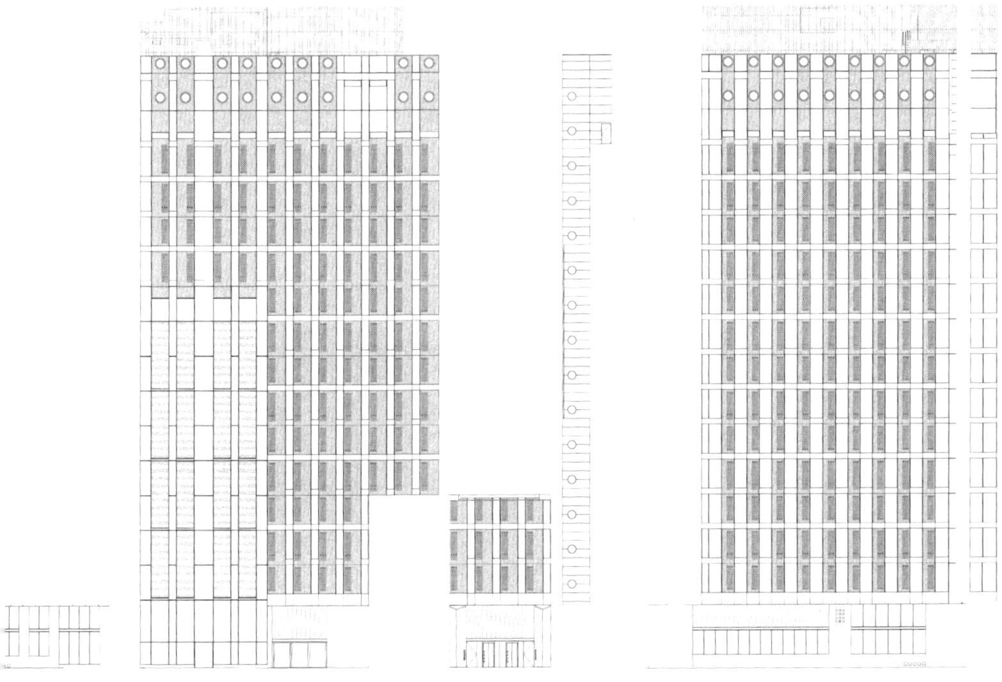

The solid elements of the facade are metal panels which, like the Jean Prouvé precedents, play with the idea of solidity with their ranks of punched 'portholes'. After refinements to the prototype, a full-size mock-up of the facade, complete with punched metal panels, was built in China during the design development and tested for wind performance and water-tightness.

At its south-east corner, the factory tower is cut in above the main entrance. This reversed out notch mimics the volume of the five-storey workspace building adjacent to it, to mediate between the tower and the low-rise elements of the White Collar campus. Rather than cantilevering out, the concrete column above is extended down as a steel totem to mark the entrance to the building, and Old Street Yard beyond.

The steel totem is painted in red oxide in a further reference to Prouvé.

The low-rise buildings have a range of brick finishes which contextualise the southern half of the site, knitting it into the grain of smaller streets to the south of the site. On the eastern side of the central courtyard, 2 Old Street Yard uses buff-coloured London stock, as does 4 Old Street Yard on Featherstone Street. The two refurbished corner buildings at numbers 3 and 5 retain their original facades. 6 Old Street Yard, an apartment building entered from Mallow Street to the west, is of a much darker brick. As with many older London alleys and rear facades, the passageway which leads into the courtyard from Featherstone Street is clad in white glazed brick.

Despite their different brick treatments, the lower-rise buildings are unified by the plant enclosure at roof level which uses the standard, British-made modular panel system by Braithwaite. Originally designed for water tanks, the sectional panels, pressed with a distinctive star motif have become icons of postwar modernism. Here, the use of these off-the-peg components gives a feeling of solidity. Braithwaite panels are also used in the downstairs reception area to clad the desk and turnstiles.

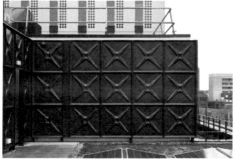

Braithwaite panels adopted for use as a reception desk (top) and as the low-rise roof plant enclosure (above).

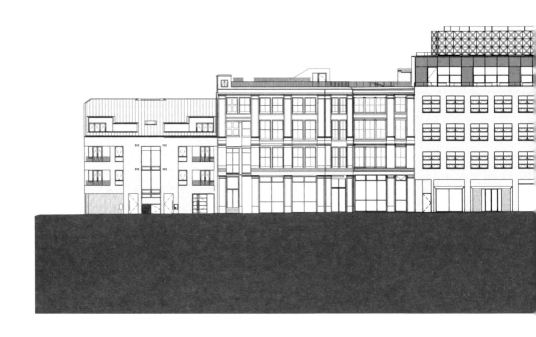

Elevations of the lower-rise buildings, unwrapped to show the varying brick treatments, and Braithwaite panels above.

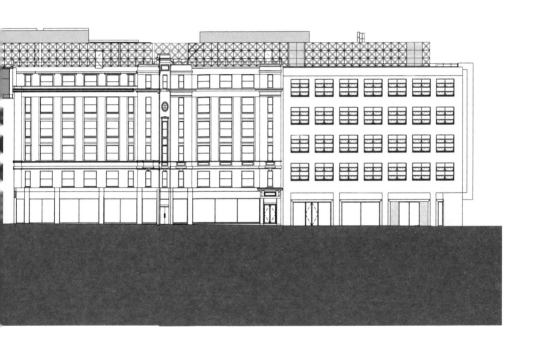

SIX BUILDINGS, ONE PLACE

OLD STREET YARD IS A NEW
PIECE OF CITY AND A NEW
POSTAL ADDRESS FOR THE
LONDON A–Z.

SIX BUILDINGS, THREE PROGRAMMES

White Collar Factory and Old Street Yard work together as a new city neighbourhood because they bring together a range of uses – live, work, play – as well as a spectrum of spaces in between where one or more programmes merge. Play mixes with work on the wifi-served tables in the courtyard; live mixes with play in the restaurants just downstairs from the new apartments. Work can be as formal or informal as the users desire, in old or new settings.

A huge below-ground studio space is the engine room of the new neighbourhood, topped by an external courtyard. Around this are six buildings: White Collar Factory (at number one Old Street Yard) and accompanying lower-rise buildings numbered clockwise from two through to six. There are tower offices of varying character, five studios and two incubator spaces in a refurbished building, eight new low-rise offices, three restaurants around the courtyard and nine new homes. The entrance hall of White Collar Factory is a new city room, and the bar at the top a private space for factory workers.

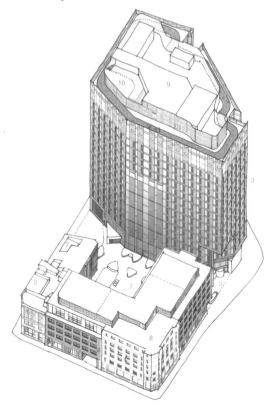

Live

1   Residential apartments
2   Residential roof terraces

Work

3   Factory floorplates
4   Low-rise factory floorplates

Play

5   Entrance hall & cafe
6   Restaurant spaces
7   Courtyard with studio space below
8   Low-rise roof terrace
9   Rooftop cafe & bar
10 Rooftop terrace
11 Running track

Axonometric view of the new neighbourhood.

ONE SPACE ABOVE

The courtyard enclosed by White Collar Factory and the buildings of Old Street Yard was designed by AHMM, with landscape architects BBUK collaborating on the planting scheme. It is laid out to reinforce the east-west route across the site as a quieter parallel to Old Street and, rather than being prescriptive, suggests spaces for the campus users and residents to rest and play. Although the yard is privately owned and managed, it is not gated and is open to the public at all hours.

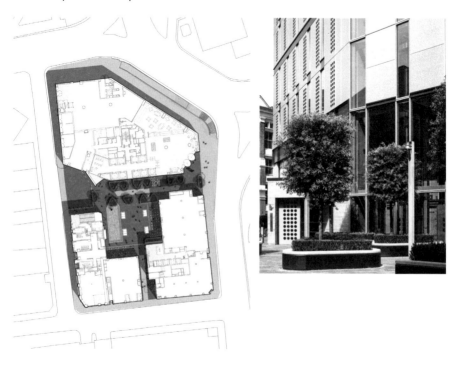

Landscape plan of Old Street Yard, showing planting defining a new east-west route; raised planters and seating in the courtyard.

Mature trees line the main pedestrian route across and help to mitigate wind from the adjacent tower, with the horseshoe-shaped planters below offering a place to sit underneath the tree canopy. There are also possibilities for informal working here, at tables and bar-type benches, all connected by external wifi. To the south, the courtyard is more open. There is a lawn to the western side with a bronze sculpture – Network – by artist Thomas J Price, who is based in nearby Bethnal Green. Along the south and eastern side of the courtyards, restaurant tables and chairs spill out into the yard. A grass-covered canopy shelters the entrance pavilion into buildings two and four in the south-east corner, while a secondary route leads through a passageway into Featherstone Street.

The hard landscaping of the courtyard is primarily of reclaimed stable yard brick, reflecting nineteenth-century courts and alleys elsewhere in the City of London. The raised planters are made from concrete with a wide edge profile to give seating, and corten steel added beneath for texture and warmth. The lamps are made from galvanised steel I-sections and are positioned to cast dappled light through the tree canopies at night. Four rooflights set into the ground surface bring natural daylight into the space below.

Network is a figurative piece depicting a man oblivious to all but his mobile phone and was originally included in The Line, a series of works brought into the public realm and placed along the line of the Greenwich Meridian as it passes through east London. It was later acquired by Derwent for Old Street Yard to reflect society's growing obsession with technology and as a reminder of the development's location off Silicon Roundabout.

CGI section showing above-ground courtyard and the basement studio space below.

ONE SPACE BELOW

A huge basement was inherited with the site, and much of this – at the perimeter of the block at least – has been used for plant and a cycle hub. However, the remaining volume has been kept and treated as a 'found space', the kind of space that is often the most memorable feature of an industrial building. These spaces, often carved out to house turbines or large machinery, give a surprise of scale and offer limitless possibilities.

At Old Street Yard, the basement was dug deeper and structural steelwork – painted pale green like the metalwork elsewhere in White Collar Factory – added to achieve a large span. The resulting volume has generous proportions – which suggest potential uses as a cafe, cinema, auditorium, pool, squash courts – but has been left for the meantime as a structural shell. It is top-lit by the openings from the courtyard above and also from the glazed lift shafts down into 'The Studio' from the White Collar tower, the movement of these lifts adding a dynamic element to the space.

Image of the space under construction.

A current idea is to transform the basement space into an impromptu food hall. This 'co-eating' space for foodies reflects the entrepreneurial spirit of the broader campus, and supports emerging talents. Start-up chefs would set up stall and prepare their food in booths around the outside of the space, with waiting staff, ingredients and general management shared collectively. There would be benches and tables for diners in the centre and a show kitchen for one-off events, with a private dining space above the main eating area. The restaurant would be open to the public, who would come into the space through a ground floor delicatessen and reception in building four, with additional direct access from White Collar Factory.

In the basement below the tower, a large two-level cycle hub has rack space for nearly three hundred bikes. Cyclists arrive at a dedicated entrance on Mallow Street, where a lobby at the corner of the apartment building leads to a wide downward stair with bicycle gutters. There are lockers for folding bikes on the first landing, and a large cycle store over both levels with a range of double and single stacked racking. Cyclists can pick up a towel from the concierge desk on each floor before moving into the banks of single-sex shower cubicles with private changing. Storage is in locker rooms with mesh cages. These are positioned above radiators, from which the rising heat dries any damp towels or cycling gear. From the main core, a gap in the concrete wall leads into the dedicated glazed shuttle lift, which delivers cyclists back into the daylight in the main entrance hall above. From here they can pass through the security line and up into their workspace.

View of the below-ground cycle hub and shuttle lift from entrance hall to cycle hub below.

CGI showing potential use of the basement studio.

THREE BUILDINGS AND A SUPERCORE

Buildings two, three and four are arranged around the south-east corner of the site. Derwent, aware of the increasing numbers of major tech players – and more recently, fintech (financial technology) companies – following the pioneering start-ups to Silicon Roundabout, wanted to ensure that the campus did not kill off the spirit of entrepreneurship that made the area so attractive. As a result, these three buildings offer workplaces of different sizes and types to suit fluctuations in the market as well as the company lifecycles of the tenants. Derwent, as investor as well as developer, tends to keep and maintain its developments, nurturing relationships with the tenants who will often move to other buildings in the portfolio as they grow. In the Old Street neighbourhood, tech companies often expand (and contract) over a very short space of time, and so generous, flexible spaces and leases without a dilapidation clause allow tenants to move in – and move on – as quickly as they need to.

Buildings two and four are low-tech, medium sized spaces appealing to SMEs (small and medium sized enterprises) with their tall ceilings, balcony space and opening, steel-framed Crittall-type windows which feel close in character to a traditional warehouse building. These new-builds hinge around building three, a retained structure on the corner of City Road and Featherstone Street which has a similar finish. Derwent has leased this building in part to Islington Council, who subsidise the space as affordable studio-style incubator offices for young start-ups.

Contrasting facade treatments for refurbished, low-rise and tower buildings.

At the inner corner of the courtyard, all three buildings share a reception area and a supercore linking to the upper floors. This core combines lifts, stair access and a fire escape, removing interruption to the floorplates above and keeping them as efficient as possible. The ground floor of each building is a restaurant, each with dual aspect to street and courtyard. These three units also feature 'soft spots', allowing direct access routes to be opened up into the double-height basement studio below, dependent on changes in programme over time.

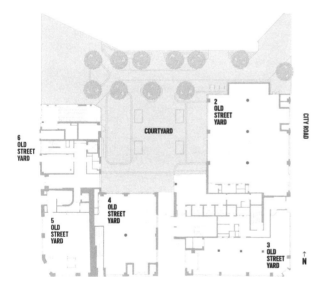

(Top) Interior views of refurbished (left) and new-build (right) low-rise offices.

(Above) Ground floor plan of Old Street Yard, highlighting buildings two, three and four.

SOMETHING OLD, SOMETHING NEW

Building five bookends the southern elevation of the campus, and is one of a pair of late nineteenth-century red brick buildings that act as a set-piece gateway to Mallow Street. It has been retained as a standalone office unit at ground floor and lower ground levels, with its own front door, high ceilings and large windows. The three floors above are given to loft apartments, with one three-bedroom unit on each floor, and all with the same high ceilings and generous sash windows. Each of the apartments has a share of the top-floor roof terrace, with the uppermost third floor apartment having its own private stair to the roof.

The sixth building of the campus, Mallow Street Apartments, is a new-build and contains six units: four two-bedroom apartments and two one-bedroom units above. Residents of buildings five and six all enter through a shared reception on Mallow Street with a seating area and mailboxes, which is glazed on the rear wall to give a visual connection through to the courtyard. The ground floor space also acts as the primary entry (via a stair) to the cycle hub in the basement. Upstairs in the new-build block, the apartments run east-west and have a dual aspect with balconies on both the front and back of the building. The top-level apartments sit under a sloping roof which is angled to reflect the rights of light envelope for the site. This pushes their living spaces away from the street and gives each a terrace, almost as large as the apartments themselves, on the front of the building.

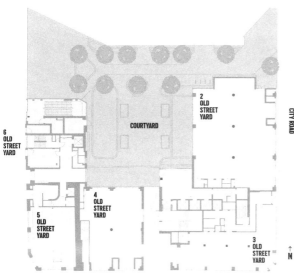

(Top) Exterior CGI view of the Mallow Street Apartments.

(Above) Ground floor plan of Old Street Yard, highlighting buildings five and six.

WHITE COLLAR FACTORY
A WALK— THROUGH

OVERLOOKING OLD STREET ROUNDABOUT, WHITE COLLAR FACTORY IS A STACK OF LONG LIFE, LOOSE FIT FLOORPLATES, SITTING ABOVE A NEW CITY ROOM AND TOPPED WITH A ROOFTOP CAFE AND BAR FOR WORKERS.

ENTRANCE HALL

The main entrance hall to White Collar Factory is a city room, a public space that anyone can enter – and draws inspiration from the large public atrium at the Angel Building. The doorway, on City Road, forgoes the grand glazed entrances of traditional office buildings for a more modest opening, marked by the red oxide totem outside, and framed in concrete, metal and cast glass. The entrance itself is through a pair of revolving doors cased in metal drums, and the feeling of compression they create maximises the surprise of the generous double-height space beyond.

Red oxide, cast glass and concrete at the main entrance to White Collar Factory.

The look and feel of the entrance hall is intended to be consistent with the factory floors beyond and so the space has been designed with the industrial turbine hall in mind. It is stripped back so the structure and services are evident and you have to come inside to get a full sense of the space.

The entrance hall is the beginning of a journey, and it offers a range of possibilities. Overlooking the roundabout there is a raised cafe area, open to the public, and contained by shallow amphitheatre-like steps which also double as informal seating. A platform lift also serves this area.

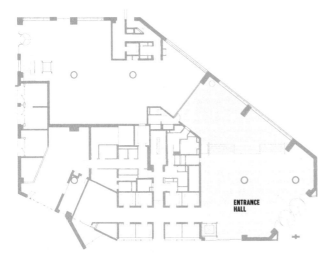

(Top) Industrial inspiration: the AEG turbine factory, Berlin (Peter Behrens, 1909) (left) and the turbine hall of Tongland Power Station (1933) (right).

(Above) Plan showing location of entrance hall on ground floor of White Collar Factory.

Interior views of the entrance hall.

FURNITURE

The lower area has two mobile work benches, designed by AHMM, which act as reception desks on the far side of the space. One is a more conventional concierge/reception, while the other is used by the building manager. Unusually, they have been brought front-of-house to enable them to help occupants work with the building. The desks are mobile and have been designed as weighty 'butchers' blocks' supported by off-the-peg metal scissor jack legs. They can be raised up and down so that receptionists can stand behind, sit at or sit on them, and have an umbilical power and data supply as well as connections to water and waste. They can be repositioned to five other locations within the hall for different events – becoming a bar or seating – or they can be removed entirely to extend the life and flexibility of the space.

The mobile work bench in use.

The upper and lower areas are both floored with saw-marked oak boards, chosen for the way they display the process of their manufacture, which will wear over time. Feature lighting on the ceiling is mounted on a yellow lighting track borrowed from the industrial production line, with loops and docking points located at various positions so that the lamps too can be repositioned for different events. To the south side of the hall are glazed doors onto the courtyard which can slide open in the summer months so that internal and external public spaces become one. A security line sits on the west side of the space protecting the entrance to the lift lobby, and adjacent to the shuttle lift to the bike hub below.

There are several pockets of informal seating within the entrance hall, and AHMM collaborated with Nicholas Chandler to select the furniture. The chairs chosen were originally designed by Pierre Jeanneret for use by civil servants and government officials in the Indian city of Chandigarh, which was designed in turn by his cousin Le Corbusier. The grandchildren of the craftspeople who first made the chair are now remaking them with the advice of their elders, and those for White Collar Factory were then upholstered in London in Bill Amberg's leather studio.

Work bench and informal seating in the entrance hall.

ART

Several artworks are also on display in the hall. There are two original Jean Prouvé louvres, found pieces of his buildings in Africa which have now become art: Sun-shutter (Cameroon, 1964) and Aluminium sun shutter (Unité d'habitation Air France, Brazzaville, Congo, 1952). Anthony Caro's piece Free fall (2013) is one of his last sculptures, its weightiness and use of materials, reflecting the boiler-house aesthetic of the building.

Furniture and found pieces in the entrance hall.

CORE

The main core of White Collar Factory sits to the south of the building and combines lift and stairs – there is also a second stair on the northern side of the building. With both cores, the idea is to encourage the building's occupants to use stairs rather than lifts where possible. They have been designed with views out, and visibility in from the floors themselves, and so are as much for breakout as they are for simple circulation.

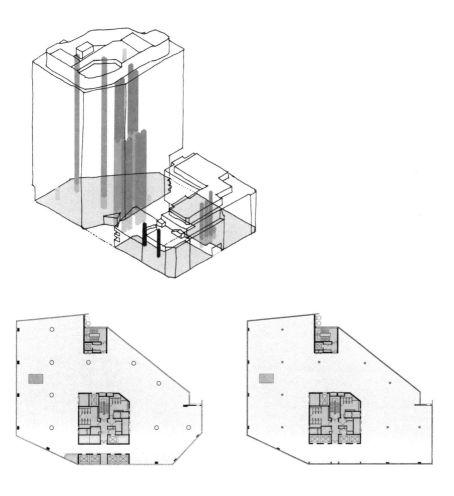

(Top) Diagram showing circulation strategy, with main passenger lifts in blue, secondary passenger lifts in yellow, residential lifts in red, and goods lifts in green.

(Above) Plans showing location of the north and south cores on lower floors (left) and upper floors (right). The upper floors gain valuable floorspace once the secondary bank of lifts falls aways at level 9.

In line with the factory-like aesthetic of the building, the lifts in White Collar Factory are standard units. At the lower lift lobbies punched porthole windows are added to the lift doors, along with full-height glazed panels in the lift cars, to give views in and out. These windows match with corresponding ones on the facade to give a view out to the city, and a sense of connection back to the courtyard. The lifts are divided into two groups: one serves the lower half of the tower (and goes no further) while the other group goes directly to the upper levels. This strategy not only minimises waiting time but also opens up valuable floor area at the perimeter of the upper floors. Tenants, if they wish, can take possession of the lift lobby on their floor, adding furniture and floor finishes to connect it more fluidly with the rest of their space.

During the morning and evening rush hours there is considerable traffic with cyclists coming into the building and going downstairs to the bike parking area, and at these times an additional lift shuttles between the entrance hall and basement to alleviate pressure on the main banks of lifts.

Lift lobbies, finished with concrete, portholes and Prouvé green paint.

The board-marked concrete which is used around the base of White Collar Factory on the street is still evident in the entrance hall, and is carried through into the lift lobby. However, in the stair and lift cores this becomes smooth, the texture being gradually lost as you move through the plan of the building. The concrete of the main stair is inlaid with metal nosings which contrast with the pale green metal balustrade. It is open to the lift lobby through pocket fire doors which are pinned back to the walls. The northern stair is expressed on the outside of the building with full-height glazing, giving views out over Old Street roundabout from the inside. The stair itself is pale green metal, which sits against the soft grey concrete walls and is lit by vertical strip lights.

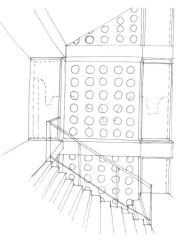

Glazing and views out from northern stair core; concept sketch illustrating relationship between stair and facade.

FACTORY FLOORPLATES

Above the entrance hall there is a mezzanine floor and fifteen levels of flexible factory floorplates (eight lower floors, five higher floors and a two floor 'penthouse') which follow the five principles of the original White Collar baseline model and prototype. Like the offices of Old Street Yard, they are designed with evolving businesses in mind, although with their generous size are more generally suited to larger organisations. The floorplates vary from a street level studio (at ground and mezzanine floors, and with its own front door) of 9,500 square feet, through three base levels and five mid-rise levels of 13,000 and 14,000 square feet respectively, to four high-rise levels of 15,000 square feet and a two-floor 'penthouse' or 'Skyloft' of 28,500 square feet which links levels 14 and 15.

One or two tenants can be accommodated on each of the factory floorplates, and if one tenant takes a whole floor the lift lobby can also become theirs, with the chosen floor finish extended throughout the whole space. Soft spots have been added to allow connections between levels to be carved out if tenants occupy a pair of floors, although these have not yet been utilised as the generous, visible stair cores provide sufficient connectivity for current tenants. On the fourteenth floor, an external pocket terrace takes advantage of the slot where the facade articulates around the north eastern corner of the building.

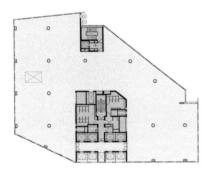 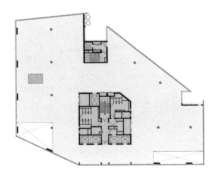

Plans of typical factory floorplates at level 8 (left) and the level 15 'Skyloft' (right).

External terrace at level 14.

The most notable feature of the factory floors is their height – 3.5 metres from floor to slab – which allows occupants to bring in self-contained systems to subdivide the space. The exposed concrete structure – walls, columns and soffit – supplies the main finish, and the inverted face of the facade is read as a darker grey. Between the solid and perforated panels there are areas of full-height glazing thee extent of which depends on the orientation (one third is glazed on the sunnier facades, while two thirds are glazed on the shadier side). Riser doors are painted in the same light Prouvé green used for metalwork elsewhere in the building. The raised access floor is left exposed (as is usual for Category A base builds) as a self-finish, and many tenants are leaving this as it is, just adding rugs on top. The lighting is bespoke, with simple tubular LED fittings based on laboratory lights suspended by metal straps from the ceiling.

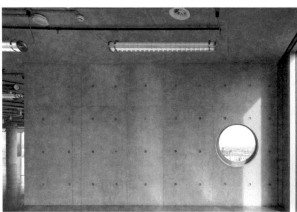

Factory finishes: concrete, Prouvé green and minimal fittings.

Factory floors: high ceilings, generous space, natural daylight.

FACTORY FIT-OUT

The first three floors of White Collar Factory have been taken by
The Office Group, which provides flexible, innovative workspace
for the start-ups and evolving enterprises which the factory
concept aims to foster. The Office Group's members are able to
choose from a range of plans to suit the lifecycle stage and work
practices of their organisation, from drop-in lounges and basic
desks in co-working areas, through to more bespoke, full-time
offices with flexible leases. The fit-out of The Office Group's floors
therefore needed to be quickly and endlessly reconfigurable to
accommodate the ebb and flow of tenants, and negate the need
to bring in outside contractors each time the space is refitted.

AHMM had, in an earlier project for Google at 6 Pancras Square,
developed a modular meeting space – the 'Jack room' – inspired
by Jean Prouvé's demountable building systems. The system,
'Jack', is built from self-structured wooden cassettes that can be
assembled, reassembled and reconfigured in a variety of ways to
create small bespoke rooms and spaces, and spatial accessories.
Each set of components comes with a manual which enables staff
to be trained to assemble them together, promoting teamwork
and collaboration.

(Top left) A demountable system: Maison du Peuple, Clichy, Paris (Jean Prouvé, 1936).

(Top right) The Jack system in use at Google's offices at 6 Pancras Square.

AHMM, having been commissioned by The Office Group to deliver the fit-out of their floors at White Collar Factory, took the Jack system and developed it further as 'Jackwall', this time basing the system on a modular partition piece rather than the box-like cassette.

The partition uses a standard 8' x 4' sheet of plywood, framed with further ply to give it depth, and 'clad' in a chosen finish – perforated plywood, blackboards and whiteboards, glass or coloured felt. Some frames hold doors, while others can be fitted with shelving. These partitions are used to subdivide the floor and are based on an exposed timber stud wall supported by a slotted metal track top and bottom. The partition cassettes are inserted and a fire batt added above to seal off the services.

The palette of finishes and manoeuvrability of the 'Jackwall' system aligns closely with the wider spirit of White Collar Factory, and does not require any specialist trades for its reconfiguration, which can be done on site by the tenant's facilities team.

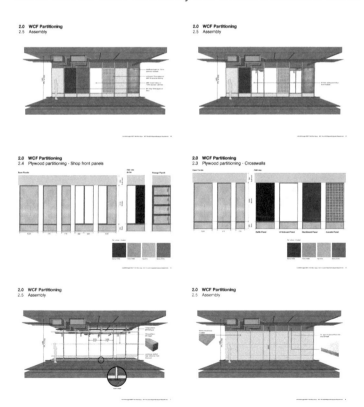

Jackwall system components, including partitions and panelling.

Jackwall in use at White Collar Factory.

ROOFTOP

The levels above the fifteenth floor serve as communal facilities
for the White Collar Factory workers. On the sixteenth floor, the
outer skin extends upwards to protect a track around the perimeter
of the building, on which the BMU (Building Maintenance Unit)
is mounted for cleaning the facade. Such cleaning only happens
four or five times each year so, in an example of convergence, with
building elements having more than a single purpose, for the rest
of the time the mounting becomes an outdoor running track for
tenants. The protective skin is punched with porthole windows
which give runners panoramic views in all directions as they
circle the track and there is a small warm-up area adjacent to
the entrance from the lift lobby.

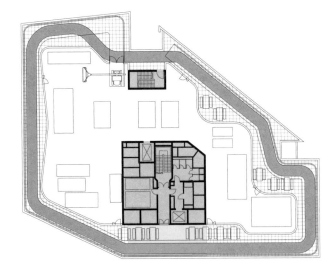

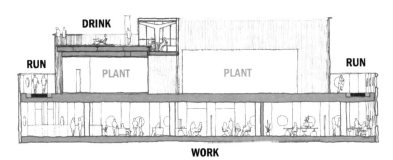

(Top) Plan of level 16, showing the running track.

(Above) Section through the upper floors, with the running track circling the plant, and bar area and terrace above.

When not in use, the BMU is hidden behind a section of the three-storey high timber enclosure which extends up from the running track. This 'hit and miss' cedar screen is 50 per cent perforate so that the plant behind it can be seen silhouetted through the gaps when viewed from a distance. This move to allow the plant to be seen is inspired by the honesty of the Manhattan skyline, where water tanks and other services are clearly visible on the rooftops.

Above here, at level 17, a contingent design for a space on top of the plant has resulted in a cafe space exclusive to White Collar workers which stands in contrast to the public entrance hall at ground floor level. From the lift lobby at level 16, a stair leads up to a rooftop bar and outside terrace. This concrete stair is lined with timber, a reverse treatment to the other landlord-maintained areas of the building which are lined with timber-marked concrete. Here the timber acts as a jacket lining for the stair, and is repeated inside the bar and on the roof terrace. The bar itself is a weathered enclosure, an indoor-outdoor room formed of a canopy with a glazed Crittall screen. The canopy is supported by Y-shaped columns, painted yellow as a further reference to Prouvé. Around the terrace, the timber plant screen is cut away by a storey to reveal views south towards the City of London.

Images of the rooftop club, supported by Y-shaped columns.

MAKING

THE MAKING OF A WHITE COLLAR FACTORY, FROM SKETCHES AND MODELS TO A PROTOTYPE; FROM MOCK-UPS THROUGH CONSTRUCTION TO THE FINAL DETAILS.

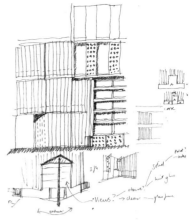
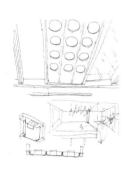
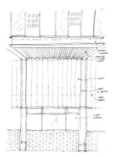
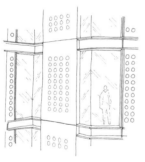
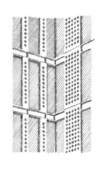
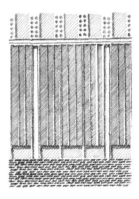
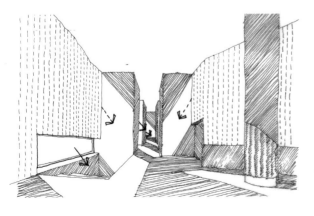

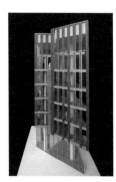

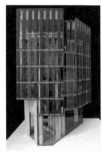

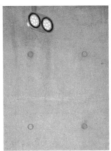

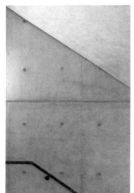

APPENDIX

TEAM CREDITS

Derwent London

Simon Silver, Paul Williams, Richard Baldwin, Benjamin Lesser, Matt Massey,
Philippa Davies, Lesley Bufton, Celine Thompson, Emily Prideaux, Rebecca Lesser,
Ed Sneddon, John Turner, John Davies, Richard Hillebron, Graham Jones,
Laura Townsend, Bob Harper – and David Rosen

Main contractor
Multiplex

Architect
Allford Hall Monaghan Morris

Simon Allford (project director), Stephen Taylor (associate director), Adam Burgess
(senior project architect), Alex Bennett, Hannah Ransom, Dan Farmer, Zoe Adeline-Lindop,
Adam Bear, Chris Pope, Liza Varnavides, Matthew Green, Bryn Williams, Matthew Jones,
Melissa Forsey, Neil Haddrill, Henry Mace, Paul Motley, Ceri Davies, Kate Rayment,
Tom Webster, Lucy Greaves, Micheal Daly, Ana Blaya, Michael Taylor, Jemma Rowe,
Iain Williams, Eleni Eforakopoulou, Lydia Robinson, Matt Gibson, Craig Shaw, Lucy Edwards,
Rhys Winslade, Sarah Baccarini, Ming Chung, Max Cotgrave, Tom Avanessian, Helen Poole,
Ellie Mackenzie, Corinne Davidson, Ellie Gregg, Clementine Seymour, Rosa Moreno Acedo,
Jonathan Hall, Paul Monaghan, Peter Morris

Engineer
Arup

Party wall surveyor
Botley Byrne

Structural and civil engineer
AKT II

Archaeology
Molas

Project manager/CDM co-ordinator
Jackson Coles

Construction legals
Speechly Bircham

Quantity surveyor
AECOM

Property legals
Macfarlanes

Building control
BRCS

Tunnel monitoring
Survey Associates

Rights of light
Gordon Ingram Associates

Brand
Studio Myerscough and Cartlidge Levene

Planning consultant
Tibbalds

Wayfinding and signage
Cartlidge Levene

Security consultant
QCIC Group

BIM coordination
BIM Technologies

FACTS AND FIGURES

Location
London, UK

Start on site
March 2014

Completion
February 2017

White Collar Factory
237,000 sq ft sixteen-storey building plus roof terrace
10,000 sq ft restaurant space
10,700 sq ft lower ground floor studio space with 6.6-metre floor to ceiling height
8,250 sq ft landscaped courtyard
40,000 sq ft flexible workspace in low-rise units
150-metre rooftop running track
276 cycle spaces
3.5-metre office floor to ceiling heights
BREEAM Outstanding / LEED Platinum

Campus
40,000 sq ft of flexible workspace in warehouse style low-rise buildings
8,250 sq ft landscaped courtyard with public art
10,700 sq ft lower ground studio space with 6.6-metre floor to ceiling height
9 characterful apartments
3 restaurant units
Estate fully wifi enabled

The White Collar Factory uses 25% less carbon over current building regulations,
a saving equivalent to:
A Boeing 747 flying from London to New York City 162 times
The mass of 16 Eiffel Towers
Driving along the Great Wall of China 76 times
Making 5,600 journeys of the entire London Underground system

White Collar Factory photography
Timothy Soar, Rob Parrish and Matt Chisnall

Aerial view
Andrew Holt

White Collar Factory in eight minutes
Home Time (workers leaving the Camperdown Mills in Dundee, 1955), John Murray/Stringer/ Getty Images

Esders clothing factory, 75-77 Avenue Philippe-Auguste, Paris, 1914, RIBA Collections

Interior of the Johnson Wax Headquarters in Racine, Wisconsin (Frank Lloyd Wright, 1940), FPG/Getty Images

Learning by inspiration
Jean Prouvé, Photographie de l'artiste/Adagp images

Prototype Maison Tropicale outside the Tate Modern in London (after Jean Prouvé, 2008),

View Pictures/Getty Images

Interior of the Larkin Building, Buffalo (Frank Lloyd Wright, 1906), with thanks to the Buffalo History Gazette

Kimbell Art Museum, Fort Worth, Texas (Louis Kahn, 1972, then Hanley Wood Architects, 2013), Richard Barnes/OTTO

Carpenter Center for the Visual Arts, Harvard University (Le Corbusier, 1963), B O'Kane/ Alamy

Interior of the Johnson Wax Headquarters in Racine, Wisconsin (Frank Lloyd Wright, 1940), FPG/Getty Images

View of the blast furnaces and the south and west facades of the Open Hearth Mills, Rouge River Plant, Ford Motor Company, Dearborn, Michigan (Albert Kahn, between 1926 and 1936), Canadian Centre for Architecture

SR Crown Hall, Illinois Institute of Technology (Mies van der Rohe, 1956), Architectural Press Archive/RIBA Collections

Project for a Concert Hall, interior perspective (Mies van der Rohe, 1942), The Museum of Modern Art, New York/Scala, Florence

Van Nelle Design Factory, Rotterdam (Leendert van der Vlugt, 1931, then Wessel de Jonge, 2004), View Pictures/Alamy

Van Nelle Design Factory, Rotterdam (Leendert van der Vlugt, 1931, then Wessel de Jonge, 2004), Kim Kaminski/Alamy

Maison de l'abbé Pierre, Paris (Jean Prouvé, 1955), Adagp images

Making city
Old Street roundabout: construction work in progress, 1971, LCC Photograph Library, London Metropolitan Archives

Old Street roundabout: construction work in progress, 1971, LCC Photograph Library, London Metropolitan Archives

Structure
Beinecke Library, Yale University (Skidmore Owings & Merrill), Ezra Stoller/Esto

Stiles and Morse Colleges, Yale University (Eero Saarinen), Ezra Stoller/Esto

National Theatre, London, Peter Cook/VIEW

Services
Boiler house, B F Goodrich Company geon plant, Louisville (Albert Kahn, 1946),
Hedrich Blessing/Canadian Centre for Architecture

Skin
Water tower and boiler house, Ipswich and East Suffolk Hospital, Ipswich
(Peter Barefoot, 1963), John McCann/RIBA Collections

Entrance hall
AEG turbine factory, Berlin (Peter Behrens, 1909), Tim Benton/RIBA Collectons

Tongland Turbine hall, Tongland Power Station (1933), Graeme Maclean

Factory fitout
Maison du Peuple, Clichy, Paris (Jean Prouvé, 1936), Architectural Press Archive/
RIBA Collections

All drawings, sketches and other photography by Allford Hall Monaghan Morris

015

Published
September 2017

Title
White Collar Factory:
A Minigraph

Author
Allford Hall Monaghan Morris /
Derwent London

ISBN
978-0-9934378-5-4

Design
Cartlidge Levene

Print
Pureprint

Specification
220 x 150mm, 168pp
Typeset in Prismatic and Grotesque
Munken Polar Rough Crisp White 150gsm
Elephant Greyboard 2250 microns
Munken Polar Rough Crisp White 300gsm
Munken Polar Rough Crisp White 150gsm
EBB Chorus Gloss 200gsm

FifthMan